10 MICE MISCHIEF

Math Facts in Action

by Caroline Stills

illustrated by Judith Rossell

SCHOLASTIC INC.

For the group I can count on: the Lazy River Writers — C. S.

For Amber — J. R.

This book matches the Common Core State Standards for
kindergarten for operations and algebraic thinking (K.OA.4).

First publishing in Australia in 2013 by Little Hare Books (an imprint of Hardie Grant Egmont)

ISBN 978-0-545-68264-0

12 11 10 9 8 7 6 5 4 3 2 1   14 15 16 17 18 19/0

Printed in the U.S.A.   40

First Scholastic printing, February 2014

The illustrations in this book were created with pencil, liquid acrylic, and collage.

10 mice wake.

9 mice tidy.

 mouse somersaults.
9+1=10

8 mice cook.

2 mice juggle.
8+2=10

7 mice wash.

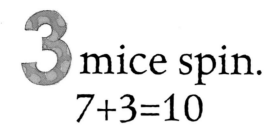

3 mice spin.
7+3=10

6 mice hang.

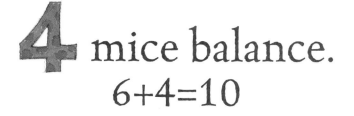

4 mice balance.
6+4=10

5 mice fold.

5 mice clown.
5+5=10

4 mice scrub.

6 mice dive.

$4+6=10$

3 mice mop.

7 mice totter.

$$3+7=10$$

2 mice dust.

8 mice build.

2+8=10

1 mouse polishes.

9 mice swing.
1+9=10

10 mice play.